Find Your Why

Joanne Mallon

vie

FIND YOUR WHY

An Hachette UK Company
www.hachette.co.uk

Vie Books, an imprint of Summersdale Publishers Ltd
Part of Octopus Publishing Group Limited
Carmelite House
50 Victoria Embankment
LONDON
EC4Y 0DZ
UK

www.summersdale.com

Printed and bound in China

ISBN: 978-1-78783-998-4

Substantial discounts on bulk quantities of Summersdale books are available to corporations, professional associations and other organizations. For details contact general enquiries: telephone: +44 (0) 1243 771107 or email: enquiries@summersdale.com.

CONTENTS

Introduction

Having a clear sense of purpose will transform your life. Studies have shown that people who know why they do what they do are healthier, live longer and sleep better at night. To live your happiest, most fulfilled life, you need to find your why.

Think of your why as your life's purpose. It's not the things you want to do or achieve; it's the reason why you want them in the first place. It's not the goal you're aiming for but the reason you get out of bed in the morning. In other words, it's the fuel in your engine.

This book contains tips, inspiration and pointers to help you work out what your unique purpose is and how you can start to live your life to be more in tune with it. Each chapter builds on the previous one to help you create an action plan. This will give you a clear sense of what your why is and how you can use it to steer your future life. Grab a notebook and pen as we start on this exciting journey of self-discovery.

Chapter 1

What is a why?

Finding your why is a process of getting to know who you are, what makes you tick and how you make a contribution to the world; it's a journey of both doing and thinking. As well as helping you to understand what a why is, this chapter will be focused on self-reflection. The clues to finding your purpose will be in your life already, so we will be taking a look back into your past. Don't be scared of this, even if you've had challenges so far. We're looking for the learning that you can take from those challenges to help you face the future from a place of strength and self-knowledge.

There is no
greater gift…
than to honour
your calling.
It's why you
were born.
And how you
become most
truly alive.

Oprah Winfrey

THINK OF THE WIDER BENEFITS

You might feel uneasy about finding your why because it feels self-indulgent to spend time contemplating what makes you, you. Isn't it selfish to think about yourself so much? Why should it matter? Aren't there more important things to fill your time with?

The answer is no: your why is an important part of a bigger picture, because it's all about what you bring to the world, the difference you can make and how that affects others. The more fulfilled you are, and the clearer your sense of purpose, the bigger that difference will be.

The danger with drifting, purposeless, through life is that eventually you may get to a point where you feel you've lost sight of the shore and wonder how you ended up with the life you're currently living. But once you've identified your purpose, you will know exactly where you've come from and where you're going. Your sense of who you are will be 3D rather than one-dimensional. You will know yourself more fully and have more to give.

FINDING YOUR WHY IS GOOD FOR YOUR HEALTH

A sense of meaning can boost your physical health and improve your longevity. Repeated studies from around the world have found that people live longer and in better health if they have a feeling of purpose in their life. This research tells us that finding your why will not only improve your well-being, but also lead to fewer strokes and heart attacks, better sleep and a lower risk of dementia and other ailments.

Much research has also found that stress has a negative effect on our physical and mental health. Knowing your purpose brings you a greater sense of happiness and calm, which means you are less likely to be a victim of the effects of stress – so think of this journey of self-discovery as essential work with tangible benefits.

When you're doing what you love, it's not exhausting at all, actually. It's completely empowering and exhilarating.

Billy Porter

SHOVE ASIDE
THE "SHOULDS"

Adopt an open mind as you start out on your journey of finding your why. Be particularly focused on how often you use the word "should". "Shoulds" are other people's goals. We're looking for an inner motivation that is individual to you and belongs to no one else.

Being connected to your inner motivation is an important part of staying true to your life's purpose. External motivators, such as deadlines, can be useful to focus your thoughts, but they work best when they're in line with your own inner drives. If you've ever procrastinated or missed a deadline, it was probably because your external motivation was too far away from your internal one. To get more in touch with your own drives, watch out for the next time you feel yourself about to say "I should" and switch it to "I need" or "I want" instead.

YOUR WHY COMES FROM WITHIN

HOW TO RECOGNIZE YOUR WHY

People often wonder how they'll know if something counts as their life's purpose. One big clue is that your why is not a person, a job, a project or a company. It's not in any outcomes that you achieve, either – those are just results. Your why lies in the journey that got you to an outcome and how it made you feel.

If you're aiming to buy a big house, reach a distance-running target or earn a particular salary, achieving those goals may not be enough to bring contentment. That stuff's not your why because those things are external results. Chances are you wouldn't necessarily be happy when you'd accomplished them if your life's purpose still remained unfulfilled.

Instead, the clue is in how you feel when you do certain things – your gut instinct that tells you that this is your mission and you're on the right track. When have you felt that time stood still? When have you felt both powerful and at peace? What work have you done that you would happily do for free? Is there a work or college project that particularly absorbed you? What was it about it that captivated you so? This is your why in action. See it and believe in it and contentment will follow.

DON'T ASK
YOURSELF WHAT
THE WORLD
NEEDS. ASK
YOURSELF WHAT
MAKES YOU COME
ALIVE, AND
GO DO THAT,

BECAUSE WHAT THE WORLD NEEDS IS PEOPLE WHO HAVE COME ALIVE.

Howard Thurman

YOUR WHY IS WHERE YOU THRIVE

As human beings, we don't just want to survive; we want to thrive. We want something deeper than simply having our physical needs met – our internal hunger needs to be fed, too. We don't merely want to plod through life, as that path often leads to disillusionment and a sense of despair.

If you sometimes feel caught up in the routines of daily living, finding your why will help you see that there is more to life than this; that you are more than the laundry you did yesterday.

When in your life have you felt that you were really thriving? Pause and think about that time now. What was happening? What makes your life worth living now? What has to happen for you to feel that you're thriving? Write down any words that stand out.

FOLLOW YOUR
PASSIONS,
FOLLOW YOUR
HEART,
AND THE THINGS
YOU NEED
WILL COME.

Elizabeth Taylor

IF IT MATTERS TO YOU, THEN IT MATTERS

Your why can be any shape or size. Your purpose doesn't have to be a grand scheme for change on a massive scale. Minor things can change the world, too. There is no such thing as a purpose that's too small; big ripples can spread from one little stone.

Don't feel you have to compare your purpose to anyone else's. Your why is unique and belongs to you. It is formed because of who you are, what you hold dear and what you bring to the world.

Anything that gives your life meaning is part of your life purpose, from the conversations you have to the books you read to the smile you face the day with. If you feel something is important and that your day wouldn't be complete without it, then it matters and deserves to have space in your life.

EVERYONE
HAS A LIGHT
TO SHINE,
AND YOUR
GLOW
IS UNIQUE

TAKE TIME OUT TO FIND YOUR WHY

Working out your why requires thought and minimal distractions. It's not a process to be hurried, so be patient if it seems unclear at first. Ask the questions and, even if you don't have answers right away, trust that your mind is working on them. You've been leading up to this moment all of your life so there's no rush.

Perhaps you could get up slightly earlier in the morning, plan a weekend away or carve out an afternoon for yourself to think about your why. When did you last take some time out that was entirely for you? When did you last go for a walk by yourself? If you can't remember, that means it's even more important to do it now. Taking time to pause will make you more able to meet your commitments when you come back to them. There's a limit to what you can do if you're exhausted and stressed out.

Use your time out to do a stock-check of how you feel at home, at work, in your relationship and in any other significant connections with the people around you. How is your health, fitness and general well-being? To what extent do you live a life you love? Which areas need the most attention? Where do you feel most out of kilter? What's the easiest thing you could do to make a positive change? When will you start?

FOCUS ON THE GOOD

A why is a positive element in your life, not a negative, so having a clear sense of it will help your mindset become more positive, too. It's an active force moving you forward, not a negative one pulling you back, which is the reason people with a clear sense of purpose feel freer and more motivated.

Some people find that embracing a positive attitude and assessing what they learn from it helps them to identify their why. Focus on what you want, rather than on what you don't. To do this, start to observe your thoughts more closely, especially if you can feel them becoming negative. Think about what you hope for rather than what you dread. If you want to make positivity a habit, challenge yourself to come up with three things you're grateful for every day, perhaps in a journal or diary, or even just on your phone.

Your present
circumstances
don't determine
where you
can go;
they merely
determine
where you start.

Nido Qubein

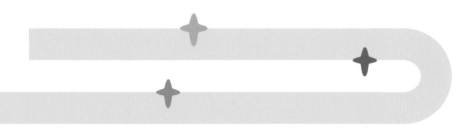

DON'T GIVE UP
ON GOALS

Goals are external: the things you want to achieve in life. Your why, on the other hand, is internal – it's at the heart of what it means to be you. But this doesn't mean that you need to give up on having goals. They can work with your why to get you to the place you want to be because they give your life some exterior focus. Targets with a timeline and definite action help you move toward the things you want.

Always keep in mind that a goal is the finish line rather than the journey, or the energy behind the journey. But know that, by aligning your goals with your why, you stand a better chance of success and of enjoying the process along the way.

FIND YOUR WHY AND YOU FIND FULFILMENT

DO A TIME AUDIT

Take a week to note down exactly how you spend your time. This is for your eyes only, so be completely honest here. There's no point in pretending that you spent half an hour meditating when you really spent three hours online.

Where are the most fulfilling parts of your day? When does time really flow so you don't look at the clock at all? In particular, note which parts of the day serve you, and which serve to undermine you. For instance, how much of your time is eaten up by things you don't really care about? How much of it was frittered away on things that don't really matter? What would happen if you didn't do those things?

Everybody needs a little downtime, but is this how you envisioned a life of purpose? Imagine that you are fully living your why – what would your time audit look like then? Given what you've learned from your current time audit, what do you plan to do differently tomorrow? Where can you eliminate some of the things that drain you and do more of the things that support and energize you?

IF YOU ARE WAITING FOR SOMEBODY TO CREATE SOMETHING, CONSIDER THAT YOU

MAY BE THAT SOMEBODY, AND THE WORLD IS WAITING FOR YOU

LET GO OF JUDGEMENT

Each person's why is unique and waiting to be discovered, so there are no right or wrong answers. Stay open to possibility rather than shutting yourself down with the reasons that something can't happen. Try new things. Be adventurous. Be playful.

A judgemental mind is a closed mind, and that will not help you right now. As you go through this book and start to get a clearer picture of your why, accept the image that begins to form. Any negative voice you hear is just your fear talking – it wants to keep you in a closed, safe space. Tell it "Not today" and stay alert and open to what might be.

OUR EXISTENCE DEPENDS UPON OFFERING THE BEST OF OURSELVES.

Nick Cave

YOU ARE **IN CHARGE** OF YOUR OWN **FEELINGS**

All we have to decide is what to do with the time that is given us.

J. R. R. Tolkien

IDENTIFY YOUR ENDGAME

In the next chapter, we'll start digging more deeply into the places where your why might be. Before we do, think about what you want to get out of that search. Why do you want to find your why? What would make that a successful process for you? How do you want to feel once you've found it? What would make this a valuable and productive use of your time?

As we've said, it's important to have an open mind on this journey, but if there is a particular solution that you're after then it's probably better to get it out in the open where it can shine rather than keeping it hidden for too much longer.

What are you really looking for here? You're more likely to find it if you define what it is before you start.

IGNORE YOUR CALLING AND IT'LL ONLY CALL LOUDER

TRUST YOURSELF

Part of the reason that it can be challenging to find your why is because it's difficult – and sometimes even an uncomfortable experience – to look within yourself and identify the recipe for your own secret sauce. You're asking yourself to have confidence in your own value. But what if you don't feel confident enough to do that just yet? The key is not to wait until you're confident enough, but rather to take action anyway and assume that it will catch up eventually.

Confidence grows in the doing; it grows from stretching beyond your comfort zone. Trust yourself that you can do this. Back yourself that, whatever happens, you will handle it. You've been in training for this all your life. As you look back over your previous experiences for the clues to your why, you will see them dropped like breadcrumbs, leading you to now. Look in the mirror and say, "I trust you." Repeat it until you believe yourself – scream it, if you have to.

Don't wait until you're confident enough to embrace your why and step fully into your life's purpose. Know that you are already enough, and that you can do this today.

Your
perfection
is inside
of you.

Oscar Wilde

LOOK FORWARD TO LIMITLESS POTENTIAL

Finding your why allows you to tap into your potential. This is the exciting part that makes it worth getting through the scary process of digging around in your life so far.

Once you know what matters most to you (and also what doesn't), you'll feel more secure as well as more able to push forward and take risks, which should mean that you achieve more in the process. Always keep pressing at the edges of your comfort zone. Be persistent and keep learning, and you'll achieve more than you think you can – as long as you take action. It's the combination of your why plus action that will lead to your greatest achievements. The fun and the future are only just beginning.

WHAT WOULD YOU BE **DOING** IF YOU KNEW YOU **COULDN'T** FAIL?

YOUR WHY MAY ALREADY BE HERE

Finding your why is not always about importing something new. Think about the little things that bring your life meaning and what they might tell you about your purpose. What is it about them that is important to you? Perhaps there's something you already do in life that gives it meaning, from your morning coffee ritual to the songs you like to play in the evening. In this case, the process of identifying your why may be more about acknowledging the importance of the things that are already there.

You may already have an inkling about what your why is, even if you're not doing it right now. It radiates out from you; it feels like a yearning. You have gold within yourself and your life so far is a map to it – you just need to follow it to the treasure.

You can, you should, and if you're brave enough to start, you will.

Stephen King

Chapter 2

How to find your why

Now that we know what a why is, it's time to do some digging into what your personal why could look like. You may find that you have more than one purpose in life or that the shape of your why changes over the years as your priorities change. The things that have been important to you so far in life may not turn out to be the same as you grow older – and this is okay, too. Your why is your totem to guide you; it's not a stick to beat yourself with. By the end of this chapter, you'll have a clearer sense of what your unique why could be.

CONSIDER WHERE YOU ARE AND WHERE YOU'VE BEEN

Once you work out your now, and how you got there, you'll be better placed to plan your future journey.

Begin by looking at the present. In your life today, what are you good at? When do you feel most at home in yourself? This could be something you do at work, at home or as a hobby. Write down five things.

What's your favourite part of the day, and why do you think that is? Write down anything that seems significant.

Next, think back over your life so far. When did you feel most fulfilled? Is there something you've been involved in that totally absorbed you? Maybe a cause you volunteered for, an important work project or a college subject? Identify what it was about this thing that engaged you so completely. As you think, write down any words or phrases that seem to stand out or reoccur. You're looking for repeating themes here.

Your why won't necessarily be the first thing you think of, so continue this process over a few days. Just like panning through grit for gold, it may take several attempts before you feel comfortable naming your why, so take your time.

WHAT DO YOU TEACH?

Another way to find your why is to think about what you give to the world and what other people learn from you. In fact, if you have an open mind, you'll either teach or learn from others in any situation – so what do people pick up from you? How do you inspire them? What do you know enough about that you can pass on your knowledge? What are your innate strengths? What have you always been good at? This could be something that other people find hard to do.

How do you help others? What do people thank you for? Think about the last time someone said thank you to you – what was that for? Write down anything that has happened three times or more.

NOTICE WHEN YOUR
HEART LEAPS UP
**IN JOYOUS
EXUBERANCE...**
IN THESE MOMENTS
THE VOICE OF YOUR
SPIRIT IS SPEAKING
DIRECTLY TO YOU.

Justine Willis Toms

WHAT DO OTHERS ASK OF YOU?

Just as you can't actually see what your home looks like unless you view it from outside, our why is such an embedded part of our psyche that we have to take a step outside ourselves to see it more clearly.

Start to see yourself as others see you. Think about how you interact with others. What do other people come to you for when they ask you for help? Is it your ideas, your knowledge or the fact that you know how to organize a great party? What have you done in your life that made other people's lives better? When people tell you that you're good at something, what is it, even if you don't really believe them? What have you been asked to do in the past that you always wanted to do more of? Write down anything that seems significant. Look for any crossover with the list of things you teach.

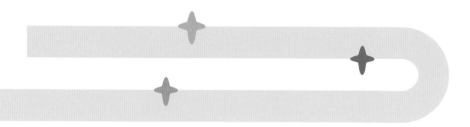

THE RIGHT TIME IS RIGHT NOW

TURN TO A TRUSTED FRIEND

When we have a natural talent for something, we often underestimate it because it feels so easy to us. We assume that everybody else must be able to do what we can do. But not everyone is good at the same things you are. If you're struggling to identify what your unique gifts might be, call in the advice of a trusted friend or relative, preferably someone you've known for a few years and who has seen you in a variety of situations.

When our light shines, we often don't realize how unique it looks to others. Ask your trusted loved one what they think your main skills or talents are. What do they think you're good at? How does this align with what you think you're good at? You may find some of what they say surprising. Ask them to remember a time when they felt that you particularly shone. What was going on then? How does this connect with what you remember about the same incident?

IT IS IN VAIN TO SAY HUMAN BEINGS OUGHT TO BE SATISFIED WITH TRANQUILLITY:

THEY MUST HAVE ACTION; AND THEY WILL MAKE IT IF THEY CANNOT FIND IT.

Charlotte Brontë

IDENTIFY
YOUR VALUES

Identifying your core, essential values is part of living a happy, fulfilled life, because once you are aware of them, you can align your life with them.

What are the essential components of life for you? Where are your deal-breakers? What do you look back on with pride? Perhaps you raised money for a cause you really care about, completed a personal challenge or got top marks in an assignment. Just like your why, your values are unique to you and are the things that you hold to be most important in life.

Make a list of ten things that are important to you. Set it aside for 24 hours to give yourself fresh perspective, then look at your list again. Pick out five that are absolutely essential to you. Compare it with the time audit you did earlier. How much of your time are you spending on things that you value? How could you live up to your values more fully?

When you
are genuinely
interested in
one thing, it will
always lead to
something else.

Eleanor Roosevelt

IF YOU COULD CHOOSE ANYTHING, WHAT WOULD IT BE?

Imagine that you won the lottery tonight and didn't have to work for money from tomorrow. What would you be doing? This is a question often asked by life coaches to get clients thinking in a wider way about the possibilities that are open to them. We often assume that our future choices have to be close to what we've done so far, when really there is a world of options out there for you. The clearer you get on what an improved life looks like to you, the easier it will be to act on it, so be as specific as you can.

Another way to approach this idea is to ask yourself: if you didn't have to do a job for the money, but you still had to fill your time, what would you do? Write down three ideas. What do they have in common? Now, how can you bring some of that to your current life?

DO
MORE
OF WHAT
MAKES
YOU
SMILE

IDENTIFY WHAT CHARGES YOU UP AND WHAT DRAINS YOU

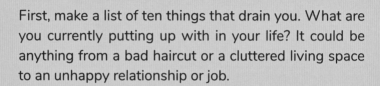

First, make a list of ten things that drain you. What are you currently putting up with in your life? It could be anything from a bad haircut or a cluttered living space to an unhappy relationship or job.

Next, make a list of ten things that give you energy. This might include exercise, nutritious food, time with friends or the satisfaction of a job well done. When does time fly for you? Which activities make you forget to check the clock or your phone?

Who – or what – would you freely give up your time for? How do you choose to spend your time when you're not at work or college? When do you feel at your happiest and most fulfilled? What is it that excites you? Think of the times when you have felt most exhilarated and write down the memory that springs to mind. Who or what inspires you? This should go deeper than just your latest hobby.

Those energizers are your why in play. Aim to do more of the things that energize you and less of those that don't. Eliminate as many of the drains as you can and you will be naturally lifted.

FIND YOUR WHY IN SERVING OTHERS

Anthropologists around the world have recognized that people are generally happiest in those moments when they feel most connected to others. So, on your journey to finding your why, look for opportunities to connect with and serve others.

Give freely of whatever resources you have. Donate your time, money or talent. Search online for volunteering opportunities near where you live or, if there's a cause you're already involved with, try becoming more immersed. This could be a way to explore a new area of life and find things that bring you a sense of fulfilment.

It is not enough to be industrious; so are the ants. What are you industrious about?

Henry David Thoreau

CONNECT TO YOUR INNER CHILD

It's time to delve a little deeper to take a look at the first green shoots of your why to understand where your motivation might have first come from. When you were a child, what did you want to be when you grew up? How did you love to fill your time? What were you curious about? What have you not done for a long time that you used to love doing when you were little?

The clues to take from your answers can be found by looking under the surface. Let's say you wanted to be a cowboy when you were younger. It doesn't necessarily mean that you should give up the office job and join the rodeo now. Instead, think about what it was about that job that appealed. Was it the variety, being outdoors, the physical challenge or maybe the chance to work with animals? How can you bring some of these elements to your life today?

TRUST THE THINGS THAT BRING YOU JOY

YOUR
FAVOURITE
THINGS

Following on from your list of the things you loved doing as a child, what else would you add to that list that you've done as an adult? Write down ten times you've felt great joy in your life. What do those experiences have in common? There are no right or wrong answers for this.

Compare your list with the things you actually spend time doing. Where does the majority of your week go? When you have free time, how do you spend it? If there's something on your joyful list that you don't do any more, think about how you could make the time for it. If you don't want to, then maybe it wasn't that important after all.

You may find that you spend your time doing things that you don't really love – and that's fine; we all have elements of our life like this. Nobody lives on cloud nine permanently. However, look out for the things that have crept into your life that take more from you than they give. Become a joy seeker. Find love. Find connection. Find happiness.

YOU ARE FULL OF PRECIOUS GIFTS – BE BRAVE

ENOUGH TO

SHARE THEM

WITH THE

WORLD

WHAT DO YOU BELIEVE IN?

Automatic writing is unfiltered writing, where you simply write or type without pausing to consider your thoughts. It's a way to get past the conscious mind and delve into the deeper contemplations lurking in our subconscious. You can use it for anything, but for now we're going to use it to dig into what you believe in. Your why is what matters to you, so your beliefs can help to illuminate what it might be.

Write the start of the sentence "I believe..." at the top of a piece of paper. Set a timer for ten minutes and start writing to complete that sentence. Don't stop writing until the timer ends. It doesn't have to make sense or be good writing. Nobody is going to look at this but you. When you've finished, read back over what you've written and ask yourself, "What do I truly believe in?" The answer might surprise you.

ONE CAN
CHOOSE TO GO
BACK TOWARD
SAFETY OR
**FORWARD
TOWARD
GROWTH.**

Abraham Maslow

DESCRIBE YOUR PERFECT WORLD

This is a fun one. If the world were run according to your rules, what would be different? What has always bothered you? What laws would you enact? What are the injustices you would fix? Where do you feel like you could make a difference? You could draw a picture to show what this world would look like. Use plenty of colour if you want. Drawing bypasses the logical brain and helps you get more creative.

Then take a step back and think about how this could apply to your current life. Where could you do something about these changes you'd like to make? You have a voice, so where will you use it and what are you going to shout about?

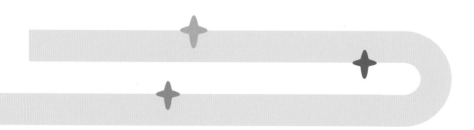

FIND YOUR
WHY
AND YOUR
HOW
WILL SOON
FOLLOW

CREATE A MOOD BOARD

If you're more of a visual person then making a mood board may work better for you than writing a list to help you identify your why. A mood board is a type of collage made up of visual elements and other objects. It's a terrific tool for enabling creative freedom and encouraging ideas to flow. Yours could be a physical board that you pin things to or a Pinterest board that works digitally (you could even use both if you want to). Set your own rules.

Gather pictures of places, people, buildings, objects, animals, quotes, plants, fictional characters – anything at all that has resonance for you – and pin them to your board. You could even add scraps of material or other objects, too. Once you have made some progress, look for repeated themes.

Try not to come to your board with the idea of creating a pattern. Instead, add things as and when it feels right and observe the patterns that naturally emerge. What are you drawn to and what doesn't merit a space? As you fill the board, stand back and look at it. What does it tell you?

As we let our
own light shine,
we unconsciously
give others
permission to
do the same.

Marianne Williamson

FIND YOUR
MOTIVATION

Do you struggle to get motivated, even with things you say you want to do? A lack of enthusiasm may be a sign that your life isn't aligned with your why.

Motivations can be positive or negative – we either want to gain or avoid something. For example: you might rush to get a report finished because you're afraid of what your boss will say if you don't. Or you might be working hard on that report because you're proud of what you've achieved and care about what you do. The first is driven by fear and stress; the second is driven by your natural enthusiasm.

Think about a task that you're struggling to complete and then think about the things you stand to gain from finishing it. Your list of values will help you here, as they can be a very strong motivational force. Look for your why within this because it will be a big part of your motivation. What do you stand to gain and how will that make a difference in your life?

TAKE THE RISK, SPEAK YOUR TRUTH AND BE FREE

HAPPY ONE-HUNDREDTH BIRTHDAY TO YOU

In this chapter, we've spent some time looking back on your past life. Now it's time to look way into the future. Close your eyes and imagine your one-hundredth birthday party. There you are, surrounded by friends and family, blowing out the candles on the cake.

What will people say about you at your hundredth birthday party? Which highlights from your life will they share? How will they sum you up? And what flavour is the cake?

To help, look at the questions we've asked earlier in this chapter. What are the common themes? Which words keep coming up repeatedly? By now, a sense of your why will be forming. What is your gut instinct telling you now?

Never lose sight of the reason for the journey, or miss a chance to see a rainbow on the way.

Gloria Gaither

Chapter 3

I have my why – now what?

Now that you've got a much clearer picture of what your why might be, the question becomes one of what to do with that information. Used wisely, it's a powerful tool to steer your life by. Having a clear sense of purpose will help you see why you do the things you do and how to cope if it feels as though life is going off course.

It's the difference between surface happiness and deep, long-lasting fulfilment, like the brief lift you get from eating a cookie versus the nourishment you get from a full, balanced meal. What will it mean to you now to lead a fully nourished life? What's the next step?

JUST
TAKE THE
FIRST STEP
AND THE
NEXT WILL
APPEAR

HOW WONDERFUL IT IS THAT NOBODY NEED WAIT A SINGLE MOMENT BEFORE STARTING TO IMPROVE THE WORLD.

Anne Frank

CREATE YOUR PERSONAL MISSION STATEMENT

Try putting your why into a statement or affirmation to help inspire you. Write it down in the form: "My why is... because..."

The first part of the statement ("My why is...") is where you state whatever it is that you bring to the party: your problem-solving ability, your creativity, your kindness, or whatever light is shining out of you. The second part of your mission statement (the "because") is where you identify the difference you make to your world and the world around you. Look back on some of your answers to the questions in Chapter 2 to remind yourself of the places where you have made a difference so far.

Don't rush it. This process will take time, quietude and space. The answers may come to you when you least expect it.

Once you've got a first draft, write it down, leave it for a week or so, then come back to it and see how you feel. Tweak it if you need to (you almost certainly will). When it makes you smile, because you recognize its truth in your heart, then you'll know you've got there.

ACT AS THOUGH...

Even if you think you've discovered your purpose, you may not be ready to jump into it, wholeheartedly, straight away. It takes courage to make a flying leap, especially if the life you want to lead is radically different from what your life looks like now. So, start by trying it on for size.

Imagine that you are already fully living your life having embraced your purpose. What's different? What would you be doing that you're not doing now? How would other people notice? Consider this picture and look for ways that you can dip a toe into it. What's the easiest change you could make right now that would bring you closer to your why? How can you best honour it in this moment?

Dare to love
yourself as if you
were a rainbow
with gold at
both ends.

Aberjhani

SHARE YOUR WHY

Once you know your why, either just in your mind or written down as a personal mission statement, it's time to reinforce it by sharing it with others. The next time someone asks what you do, don't simply reel off a job title. Instead, tell them about your purpose. You don't have to declare it like an advertising slogan; just talk about the stuff you love to do and why that is.

Don't be surprised if you feel exposed and vulnerable the first few times you share your why with somebody else. It speaks to the core of who you are, your sense of worth and what you bring to the world. Self-esteem often wobbles, and it can feel scary to stand on that precipice. Be brave. Be vulnerable. Put yourself out there so like-minded people can recognize and connect with who you really are.

FIND YOUR WHY AND YOU FIND YOUR SOUL

USE YOUR WHY AS YOUR GUIDING STAR

From now on, take care to make decisions with your why in mind. When you're unsure about something, always ask yourself: does this support my purpose or take me further away from it?

Your why is the most important thing in your life because it supports and drives everything else. Think of it as your centre and keep coming back to it. This isn't about being selfish and only doing things that serve your own ends. As we've said from the start, your why is what allows you to achieve a deep sense of fulfilment – and it tends to serve others well, too. So, as you live up to your why, not only are you helping yourself, you're also helping the people around you. If something is intrinsically selfish and doesn't have a wider benefit – or even has a negative effect on someone else – then that's usually a red flag that it's not your why.

You'll find that even dilemmas become easier to navigate once you know your why, because you can simply ask yourself if each situation fits with your purpose or not. And once you've made that decision, then you'll know what action to take next.

WE BEGIN TO FIND
AND BECOME
OURSELVES WHEN
WE NOTICE HOW
WE ARE ALREADY
FOUND, ALREADY

TRULY, ENTIRELY, WILDLY, MESSILY, MARVELLOUSLY WHO WE WERE BORN TO BE.

Anne Lamott

FIND YOUR TRIBE

Once you identify your why, others with a similar purpose may show up, or maybe they were there all along and you're only noticing them now. The people we are drawn to can tell us a lot about ourselves. Who do you admire? What qualities do they have? What is it about the people you admire that speaks to you? There's a reason we're drawn to particular people, and finding your purpose can tell you why.

Look for like-minded individuals that your why can connect you to. This could be someone with a similar purpose to you, or perhaps someone who has complementary talents. For instance, if you're a person who's very good at noticing the little details, you might benefit – in work or life – from teaming up with someone whose skills are in seeing the bigger picture. This may mean deepening relationships you already have or finding ways to meet new people.

The mystery of human existence lies not in just staying alive, but in finding something to live for.

Fyodor Dostoyevsky

BE

BOLD.

BE

BRILLIANT.

BE

BRAVE.

THERE IS NO GREATER AGONY THAN BEARING AN UNTOLD STORY INSIDE YOU.

Zora Neale Hurston

FIND PURPOSE IN THE SMALL THINGS

Acting on your why doesn't necessarily lead to a big upheaval in your life. Not everyone will end up leaving home to join the circus. Simply start where you already are and make a point of aligning your existing life with the things that are important to you.

Look for ways to honour your purpose in your day-to-day activities. For example, if you've discovered that you're a particularly good problem-solver, or that you're organized, or you make people laugh, find ways to do those things more often. By doing so, not only will you find out whether this really is your purpose, but you'll also feel good the more you lean into it, which will give you the confidence to embrace it even more. This will make it easier for you to apply your why more widely in your life. Every long journey starts with a walk.

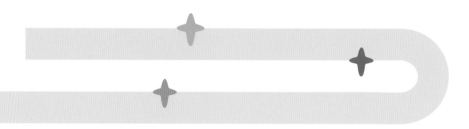

EVERY 100-FOOT OAK TREE WAS ONCE A SEED

DEVELOP YOUR PASSION

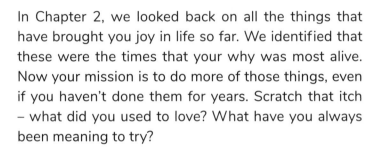

In Chapter 2, we looked back on all the things that have brought you joy in life so far. We identified that these were the times that your why was most alive. Now your mission is to do more of those things, even if you haven't done them for years. Scratch that itch – what did you used to love? What have you always been meaning to try?

It could be time to take an evening class or register for a training course at work. Perhaps you'd like to visit somewhere you've never been before or join in a new social activity. If there's a passion you already make time for, what would be the next step to get better at it and expand your involvement?

Make an appointment this week to do something that's either an existing or a potential new passion. Put it in your calendar so it definitely happens. Don't say that you'll do it "someday". Your why starts now.

WHAT'S IMPORTANT TO YOU?

Let's look at how your why and its supporting values show up in your life. Think about the last time you did something that you felt was important. This could be anything from a memorable walk, to an exciting event, to attending an appointment you were scared to make but are now glad that you did. Look back over your calendar for the last few months and see which days are most memorable. If you don't keep a diary, start one today and make a note of how you spend your time and when you do things that you feel are important.

How did that significant event come about? Who was there that made it so special? What was your contribution? Could you do it again? Making space for the things that are meaningful to you will help you to feel more fulfilled and purposeful. It's likely that the things we find most meaningful and memorable align with our values and our why, so making space for these will help you to feel more fulfilled and purposeful.

If we have
our own "why"
of life we
shall get along
with almost
any "how".

Friedrich Nietzsche

DON'T GET DERAILED

Even though you've identified your life purpose, you may find yourself drifting away from it sometimes. This is what happens when we get swept up in other people's values, goals and passions. Be wary of this. It's not that theirs are less valuable than yours, but they are different, and you deserve to stay on your own path.

Many things can distract us from focusing on our why. Don't be seduced by money and status – that stuff only goes so far; don't settle for a life half lived, because that's what yours will be if you lose sight of your purpose and start living somebody else's; don't get dazzled by the shiny things in life. Take some time to yourself every so often to check in with how things are going and ask whether you need to make some changes to bring yourself back to your own unique purpose.

BELIEVE IN YOUR WHY. BELIEF HAS POWER.

LEARN TO LET GO

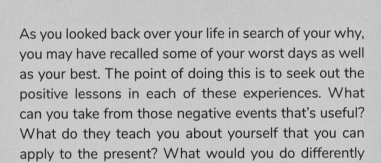

As you looked back over your life in search of your why, you may have recalled some of your worst days as well as your best. The point of doing this is to seek out the positive lessons in each of these experiences. What can you take from those negative events that's useful? What do they teach you about yourself that you can apply to the present? What would you do differently next time?

When you're examining your past, you might become fixated on the negative side of your experiences. However, continuing to carry these things that drag you down is like carrying a bucket of poison everywhere you go. It doesn't help. It slows you down. It won't serve you and it isn't part of your why.

Let it go. Make a conscious decision to set that bucket down now and walk away. Take only the positive learning with you from each experience from here on in. This may be tough to do, but you *can* do it.

FINDING YOUR WHY IS NOT ABOUT FINDING THE BEST PATH;

IT'S ABOUT CREATING THE BEST JOURNEY

ENJOY THE ENERGY SURGE

You will probably find that identifying your purpose gives you a lot more energy. You will wake up feeling more alive, even though you may be working harder, and at the end of the day you won't feel exhausted because you will be less stressed. (By the way, if these things aren't happening then this is a clue that maybe you aren't quite living your purpose just yet.)

What to do with all this energy? Don't take it as a cue to push yourself more and more. Take care of yourself both physically and mentally. You're carrying precious gifts within you, but you need to look after them so they can be of the greatest benefit. You may be worried that a busy life means that burnout is inevitable, but it doesn't have to be if we look after our physical and mental health along the way. Instead, enjoy the ease of being in flow with who you really are.

A bird doesn't sing because he has an answer, he sings because he has a song.

Joan Walsh Anglund

LISTEN TO FEEDBACK

As you start to live your life in alignment with your purpose, stay alert to the feedback you're getting, both verbally and non-verbally. Others may notice if you start to shine (although, if they don't, that's okay, too). Expand your network and be open to conversations with new people. Surround yourself with positive people who care about a sense of purpose.

Also be alert to your own inner feedback. What is your gut instinct saying to you now compared to in the past? When does it tell you that you're on the right track? Do how you dress, how you carry yourself and how you treat yourself reflect your newly engaged sense of purpose? Be kind to yourself: you're doing good work.

YOU'VE GOT THIS!

TAKE
A BIG
LEAP

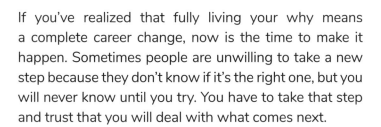

If you've realized that fully living your why means a complete career change, now is the time to make it happen. Sometimes people are unwilling to take a new step because they don't know if it's the right one, but you will never know until you try. You have to take that step and trust that you will deal with what comes next.

Although many people believe that when one door shuts another door opens, in general most of us would prefer it if the new door was already open before the old one closed. Sometimes this will be possible, but often it will not, and you have to be brave. This is where you will be carried by a secure knowledge of your strengths and a firm sense of self-belief.

If your big leap involves a brand-new job in a brand-new industry, one way to get there is by moving your current job to the new industry, and then stepping across into a new role from there. If you want to commit to your passion project full-time, you may have to run the old and the new in parallel for a while until you can leave your day job. There is always a way, as long as you take action and go for it.

UNTIL ONE IS COMMITTED, THERE IS HESITANCY, THE CHANCE TO DRAW BACK, ALWAYS INEFFECTIVENESS.

William Hutchison Murray

MATCH YOUR WHY TO YOUR GOALS WITH INTENTION AND ACTION

We noted right at the start of this book that your why and your goals are not the same thing. Your why is the fuel that takes you there and your goals are your end destination. But you can use your knowledge of your why to help you achieve your goals. This is done by making sure that any action you take (and it all comes down to action) is in alignment with your why.

Think about your goals in the context of your why. Do the two fit seamlessly together? How will you have fulfilled your purpose if you achieve that particular outcome? What will it mean to you?

FIND YOUR **HAPPY** PLACE, THEN **LIVE** IN IT

WELCOME YOUR WHY
IF IT'S ALREADY HERE

When you did the work in Chapter 2 to help discover your why, you may have felt a rush of recognition as you found that your why was closer than you expected. Perhaps you were already living your why but just hadn't articulated it yet. In which case, congratulations! No big upheaval for you. You lucked out already.

This isn't your cue to lie back on the sofa and relax because you've got everything sorted. Life is always changing, and it will never be the same as it is today. People and jobs will come and go, but you will stay constant at the heart of it all. Be appreciative, not complacent. Be awake, not sleeping. Embrace the changes that life brings your way as a chance to grow and stretch.

Nothing is
impossible.
The word
itself says
"I'm possible."

Audrey Hepburn

Chapter 4

Looking to the future

It would be naïve to think that, once we've found our why, that would be everything wrapped up and sorted for an easy future. If only it were that simple! Many things in life ebb and flow, including confidence, self-esteem and your sense of purpose. In this final chapter, we look at how you can stay positive and resilient, even when life is challenging you to be anything but. Life may never be entirely plain sailing, but hang onto the rudder of your why and you will get through the choppy bits.

LOOK TO YOUR SUPPORT SYSTEM

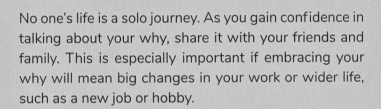

No one's life is a solo journey. As you gain confidence in talking about your why, share it with your friends and family. This is especially important if embracing your why will mean big changes in your work or wider life, such as a new job or hobby.

Talk to the people in your support system about your why and how you intend to follow it. You could also think about how your purpose could be used to support others. Now that you know what you've got to give, who are you going to give it to? Maybe you could share how you found your why and help those around you find theirs, too.

You may need to convince others that it's okay for your path to be different from theirs, or different from what you have been doing before. Part of this may involve letting go of relationships that aren't supportive, which can be difficult. However, it's okay to do this with love if it's not serving either of you. The key is to move on in a positive way.

BELIEVE IN YOURSELF

We all have darker days when we think we can't do something. And yet, time passes, and somehow we manage it. Think back over some of the occasions when life wasn't so dark to remind yourself why you're on your particular path in the first place. Whatever you focus on in your life takes up greater mental energy, so look for the positives and you will find more of them. Consider what you're going to learn from your current experience, even if it's negative. What will you take from these dark days that will make you stronger next time?

Another technique to bring yourself out of a darker patch is to challenge negative thought patterns. Be aware of when you're assuming something will fail before you even start. Keeping a gratitude journal can be great for this, as it helps you to make positive thinking into a habit. Note down three good things about your day every evening and soon you will move your mindset in a more optimistic direction.

Life is always either a tightrope or a feather bed. Give me the tightrope.

Edith Wharton

TIME TRAVEL

To gain a new perspective on your life today, write a letter to yourself from the future. Date it ten years from today. What will you be looking back on and celebrating? What are the values that you are proud to have lived by? How did you know that you had been true to yourself? What advice does future you have to give to the you of today? Don't worry if you're not entirely sure what to write. It's okay to begin with a broad-brush sketch. Start with a wide-angle view and the details will soon appear.

If you feel like taking this exercise to its ultimate limit, another approach is to write your own obituary. How do you want to be remembered? In the story of your life, what were the highlights?

DON'T WASTE YOUR ENERGY THINKING ABOUT "WHAT IFS"; FOCUS ON WHAT IS

HAVE FAITH IN YOURSELF

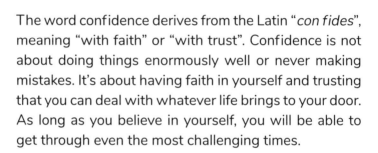

The word confidence derives from the Latin "*con fides*", meaning "with faith" or "with trust". Confidence is not about doing things enormously well or never making mistakes. It's about having faith in yourself and trusting that you can deal with whatever life brings to your door. As long as you believe in yourself, you will be able to get through even the most challenging times.

To restore your confidence, you could retreat to something that you feel naturally good at. It could be anything from riding a bicycle to making a cake. This will remind you that you can be confident in the small ways, and therefore you have the potential to be in larger ways, too.

Think of a newborn baby: freshly arrived into the world and curious about life. Newborns are effortlessly confident because it has never occurred to them to be anything else; they assume that the world will respond to their needs and support them. You once had that effortless newborn confidence and if you had it once then you can get it again.

IF YOU ORGANIZE YOUR LIFE AROUND YOUR PASSION, YOU CAN TURN YOUR PASSION INTO YOUR STORY

AND THEN TURN YOUR STORY INTO SOMETHING BIGGER – SOMETHING THAT MATTERS.

Blake Mycoskie

WAVE
YOUR FLAG

Earlier, we looked at how you could turn your why into a sort of personal mission statement, and how it's a good idea to start telling people about your why once you've identified it. By doing this, we take our why out into the world and it gathers more energy than it would if we had kept it a secret. Everything expands when you share it.

Think of your why as a flag you're waving that says, "I'm here and I have value." Your why is something to cling onto when life gets tough. If you ever ask yourself, "Why am I doing this anyway?" then you already have the answer. Be proud of the colours of your flag and wave it high.

HIDE NOT YOUR TALENTS, THEY FOR USE WERE MADE. WHAT'S A SUNDIAL IN THE SHADE?

Benjamin Franklin

TRUST YOUR GUT, NOT YOUR FEAR

Be aware of the difference between gut instinct and fear. They can often feel the same – an indefinite feeling of "knowing" that comes from your body. But your gut will pull you toward things, whereas your fear will often push things away. When fear shows up, we make excuses about why something can't happen. For instance, perhaps you're worried about how people will judge you or that you're not strong enough to carry a task through to the end.

Fear is often particularly evident when we're on the brink of a major change or breakthrough. This is the feeling of your comfort zone expanding. It always feels scary when you're at the edge, but pressing on despite the fear is what will lead to progress.

IT'S
OKAY
NOT
TO
FEEL
OKAY

CHANGE
YOUR MIND
BUT KEEP
YOUR WHY

Your life circumstances and priorities will change throughout your life, so it's okay to take a new path if you need to. Give yourself permission to alter your destination or to be wrong. The course of your life will take many turnings and sometimes what feels like a misstep can actually be taking you to a better place.

When things do change, the core elements of your purpose might do so, too. Then again, they may not vary very much at all. It may be that you keep your purpose but apply it in a different way, with new projects, new situations and new people.

As you define your purpose, you also define the things that are important to you. By implication, you'll also see what is not important to you. You'll know what to move toward and what to avoid. You'll know when to change and when to keep going. Be flexible but still true to yourself. Be agile but responsive to life. Take a new path and delight in the possibilities.

MAKE TIME FOR SELF-CARE

Looking after yourself is essential, not only so that you stay feeling your best both physically and emotionally, but also to ensure that you can pursue your why without feeling burned out. After all, you are your own support system. Eat nourishing food; drink water; go outside in nature every day if you can; move your body; make sleep a priority. These are the basic building blocks of good health, which are so simple that we sometimes overlook them.

Finding your why will give you more energy than you had before, but it won't turn you into a superhero. Seeing where you fit into the wider picture will help you appreciate yourself and treat yourself as someone valuable with precious gifts to give.

You have to
keep the fire
under you,
because that's
what makes
you better.

Reese Witherspoon

EMBRACE AND REFRAME FAILURE

Not everything you embark on will be a resounding success. Making mistakes is part of being human (and, as you're not a robot, you will be human many times in your life!). Although it can be tough when you're in the middle of things going wrong, when we look back on our mistakes, we can often see how they were an inevitable step on the path leading us to a better future.

The important part of failure is to learn from it and use it to make a plan for whatever you will do differently next time. Think about what you regard as your worst failure or mistake in life. Write down five things that it has taught you. This is its value. This is what will help you do better next time. This is what you take with you into the future: learnings, not baggage.

FOCUS ON WHERE YOU'RE GOING RATHER THAN WHAT IS STANDING IN YOUR WAY

WHEN LIFE DOESN'T FOLLOW THE PLAN

Every life is a map of the unexpected. Life throws all kinds of surprises at us that we never would've thought we could handle had we seen them coming. And yet we do handle them because we are deeper wells than we thought we were.

If your life goes off course and you find yourself moving away from your purpose, take some time out to assess what's going on. Perhaps you have another purpose now; perhaps you need to make some hard decisions and radical changes in your life; perhaps you'll find a new purpose to expand on your original why; perhaps you simply need to focus on better self-care while looking after those around you.

Take time to think and slow your pace. Stay nourished. Your why will still be there for you when you're ready to embrace it again, just as it was always there before you could say what it was.

TRYING TO FIT IN JUST GETS YOU BENT OUT OF SHAPE

– YOU ARE

PERFECT

JUST AS

YOU ARE

QUESTIONING YOUR WHY

It's natural to feel lost sometimes, or to question whether the why you're pursuing really is your true life's purpose. If you feel this way, the key is to keep your mind open and not to be afraid of asking questions. If you find yourself doubting your why, perhaps you need to spend more time refining it. Remember that there isn't necessarily one "true" life purpose; something might be true at one point in your life, but something else might be true later on.

Go back to some of the questions we asked in Chapter 2. Your subconscious will have been mulling on these as you were focusing on other things, so your answers could be different this time. Return to your list of values and the things that are most important to you. Where are they in your life now? This is a lot for you to chew over, so take your time. Keep probing and the way forward will become clear.

CHERISH
YOUR
ONE SHORT
AND
PRECIOUS
LIFE

USE AFFIRMATIONS

An affirmation is a short, positive sentence that you can use to help bolster your self-belief, such as "I live in an abundant universe" or "I am enough." Saying or reading an affirmation repeatedly will help you to feel calmer and more focused. It can be very effective to repeat yours in front of the mirror, looking yourself in the eye as you speak. You could also write it out on a card or sticky note and stick it where you'll see it often.

Check out the motivational quotes and statements in this book – maybe one of these could be a new positive affirmation for you – or write your own. You'll get the biggest benefit by checking in with your affirmations in the morning, because this starts your day on a positive note.

BELIEVE IN YOURSELF AND OTHERS WILL BELIEVE IN YOU, TOO

REMEMBER WHY YOU STARTED

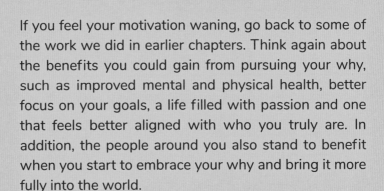

If you feel your motivation waning, go back to some of the work we did in earlier chapters. Think again about the benefits you could gain from pursuing your why, such as improved mental and physical health, better focus on your goals, a life filled with passion and one that feels better aligned with who you truly are. In addition, the people around you also stand to benefit when you start to embrace your why and bring it more fully into the world.

Have you noticed any improvements in your physical and mental health since you started thinking about and looking for your why? Write down any that occur to you. Having a list of tangible benefits that you can look back on can give you a boost when you need it and remind you of all the great things you have already achieved.

Ask what your journey has taught you about yourself so far. What do you intend to do with that knowledge? Taking action is the key to making your work on your purpose meaningful and transformational. What will you do now and when will you start? Make a list of three things you are passionate about and aim to do one of them by the end of this week.

Read books.
Care about
things. Get
excited. Try not
to be too down
on yourself.
Enjoy the ever-
present game
of knowing.

Hank Green

LET GO OF PERFECTION

Perfectionism is not your friend. For something to be perfect, it has to be completely finished. It can't get any better or worse; it's as good as it's going to get.

We often try to apply perfectionism to our own lives, but life is never static to allow this. Life is messy and often raw at the edges. It never stays still – in fact, it changes every day. By aiming for perfection, you are shooting for a goal that doesn't exist. You're setting yourself up for inevitable failure and a feeling of being unfulfilled. Your why isn't perfect – it's a light to guide you, rather than a standard to be met. It's as delightfully human and marvellous as you are.

Aim for your own personal best – a gold standard – rather than perfection. Then you have a goal that's within reach, and that you can be proud of when you achieve it.

IF YOU ASK
ME WHAT I
CAME TO DO
IN THIS WORLD,

I... WILL ANSWER YOU: I AM HERE TO LIVE OUT LOUD!

Émile Zola

YOU DON'T HAVE TO BE PERFECT TO BE AMAZING

THE
BEGINNING
IS ALWAYS
TODAY.

Mary Shelley

ALL
YOU
NEED
IS
YOU

Conclusion

Everyone has their own journey to finding their why, and each path is valid. It may come to you in a lightbulb moment or it may take longer to mull over and so appear gradually. There is no right or wrong way to do this. There is only your way.

With the help of this book, you may have already found your why, or, if you haven't taken any action yet, now is the time to go back and look at some of the suggested notes and lists. Even just by taking the time to read this far, you've already made an important declaration that you're ready to invest in the future and find the things that will bring you true fulfilment and happiness.

Every day is a fresh chance to embrace your why or to progress toward defining it. Start from here, keep moving and you will get there. Above all, do your best in the present moment. Find your why and be proud of it. Commit fully. Be totally engaged. Sing your song.

If you're interested in finding out
more about our books, find us on Facebook
at **Summersdale Publishers**, on Twitter at
@Summersdale and on Instagram at
@summersdalebooks.

www.summersdale.com